echolalia

I0892095

echolalia

poems by Deborah Bernhardt

Four Way Books
New York City

Distributed by
University Press of New England
Hanover and London

Editorial Office
Four Way Books
POB 535, Village Station
New York, NY 10014
www.fourwaybooks.com

Library of Congress Catalogue Card Number: 2004114708

ISBN 1-884800-72-6

Cover art: Rebecca Strzelec, *Apology Brooch* (front) and *Line Brooch* (back) from *The Shorthand Series*, 2004, Fused Deposition Modeled ABS Plastic and Medical Adhesive. Courtesy of the artist.

Book cover design: Cubanica

This book is manufactured in the United States of America and printed on acid-free paper.

Funding for the Intro Prize in Poetry was provided in part by a generous donation in memory of John J. Wilson.

Four Way Books is a not-for-profit literary press. We are grateful for the assistance we receive from individual donors, government arts agencies, and private foundations.

Distributed by University Press of New England
One Court Street, Lebanon, NH 03766

[clmp]
We are a proud member of the Council of Literary Magazines and Presses.

Grateful acknowledgment is made to the editors, readers, and staffs of the following publications in which these poems, sometimes in earlier versions, first appeared:

Barrow Street: "Landscaping"

can we have our ball back?: "The Hereafter Has Been Modified as Follows"

columbia poetry review: "Latin Roots Sui and Cidium"

Court Green: "Sometimes a Septum Almost Deviates"

Cue: a Journal of Prose Poetry: "The Kiss" and "Lethal"

Fence: "Apology Is Red up Like This," "Scanning, with the Eye," and "There Is No Towards"

Indiana Review: "Temple Grandin's Squeeze Machine"

Pog 2: The Second Anthology of Writers and Artists Appearing in Events Sponsored by Pog: "Made Out of Sixes"

Quarterly West: "Death and Saucepan," "*Happy Living! A Guidebook for Brides*," "To Lisa: We Descend from Worried Mothers," "Replacing a Threshold," and "What Lisa Thinks"

Shankpainter 41: "Text" and "Fractal"

Grateful thanks to the Wisconsin Arts Board, the Wisconsin Institute for Creative Writing/Jay C. and Ruth Halls Fellowship, the Fine Arts Work Center, Provincetown, Penn State Altoona, the University of Denver, and Writers@Work for fellowships and dear friendships that made possible the completion of this book.

Thank you, with admiration, to Jon Anderson, Barbara Cully, Mark Doty, Rikki Ducornet, Cornelius Eady, Thomas Lux, Jane Miller, Tenney Nathanson, Steve Orlen, Bin Ramke, Boyer Rickel, and Cole Swensen, without whom I could not have written this book.

Thank you to my students for reading poetry with me.

A debt of love to Julian P. Billups, Eric Burger, Jeremy Bushnell, Lisa Coffman, Maggie Golston, Kat McLellan, Antonio Rauti, Kate Rosenberg, and Rebecca Strzelec for their insight and generosity.

To Julian, for carriage of every page except this one.

Endless gratitude and thanks to Marianne Boruch, Four Way Books, Sally Ball, Martha Rhodes, and Jason Schneiderman for the thing itself.

To my parents, with love.

Dear Unconscious scatter syntax

scythe mower surrender hereafter.

—Susan Howe

for Michael J. Patrick

CONTENTS

&

SCANNING, WITH THE EYE,

on your sort-by-word setting, a book of poems.
If you like words, you favor a kinda kind of words.

Latinate—that could be a predilection.
Or Gen X Froot Loop Soho words. Or lots

of esses, in general, could get to you, like *the suss*
of immense stockings. Or maybe

unfurling combinations: hybrid high bird, vis-à-vis, visa visa, arriba arriba.
I think one of the addressees in this here poem

might like *fire-fangled feathers dangle down.* F-stop. F-forward,
to the end of the mind, all the way up to preference Q,

maybe even all the way up to R (no one ever knows a mind
all the way to Z). (cf. V. Woolf). Not even You, as in Thou. Skimming,

running a hand over the peaks of mountain ranges
to see if they are loveable hikes. Above him

his desire spins. He rests, periodically—between taste and budding—
so he won't careen. Much as I'm a safety girl, I encourage

hiking toward the end of the mind or at least the tip of the tongue.
Now I'm here, and you're here, and you is
the most recent semiavailable you, maybe even the one—

we're tired of hearing about your boyfriends, Deborah,
can't you write about something important, look around you, think of
Czeslaw Milosz.

Come now.
Let's pursue something else,

now then, that's a bright, bright Mars rising, and although
you won't know the difference between my lovers   and God

we see the difference between Mars and a star
by measuring brightnesses. Mars—close-up, like we saw in Nat Geo Magazine—

is a desert, pocked.
His toothmark on my lip. You know it's not my own
by the orientation of the crescent.

Let's steal something from him. (You! Everyone not him!)
Now him is Miss Stein. *He he he*
he and he and he and and he and he and he and and as
and as he and as he....you could know perfectly well a sequence of fairly
perpetual assertions of a single masculine subject and that whatever is being
done by Picasso he is doing it simply and nakedly
as or qua a very singular very masculine very active subject. That his
Spanish giggle sounds like the English word for the essence of the man
and his work is just one of the miracles,   she said
in her   *interview.*

Don't dislike him, our male character here.
Our composite.
To resume: two fictions going on. Look at

the Rosetta stone of encircled red wine. I gave, for this, the nicest glass I own,
as if the speaker were half empty in love with the addressee. Surface

of the wine: a pocket-sized etch-a-sketch.
In order to take possession of the moonlight.

No, it wasn't possession.
When you tilted the glass/when he did tilt the glass

he saw the moon that he could love,
full loveable moon on wine,
moonlight rippling the calligraphy over merlot surface,

and I read over your shoulder,
and you showed me how to position my own glass, so I can write on my own
surface
of wine, and this makes us both feminists,

and how did he know just what I would like indoors,
and that is one of the ways you got into the poem, under the skin,

the ten pale quarter moons at the roots of my fingernails reddening
at the sight of him. My system goes *pah!* as if

two guys in Aerosmith shirts are screwing up in the amp department,
as if the music were so loud your lips were on my ear,

and I have lost the way here, the conceit of the thing and the grammar.
What is loveable about speakers. Who is loveable after hours. Which words.

TEXT

Forever, the deeper opposite of a picture,
Your leaves, the part of you
That the sea first talked to.
—"Marconi's Cottage," Medbh McGuckian

Stanching with bedsheets. The Rome of his chest, the alterable history.
A shutter, said Cartier-Bresson, requires *a velvet hand, a hawk's eye.*
Our only moment of creation
is that 1/125th of a second
when the shutter clicks, the signal
is given, and motion is stopped. "The" phone call,

the decisive moment—epiphanic uncropped prints that include
the black border of the negative. When the star said
I'm thinking about killing myself his love interest said
No, you can't, which isn't a strong rhetorical strategy.

Welcome to the Biology Lab.
parasites of the eastern chipmunk and other squirrels
the niche space in which they live

It's when I'm almost asleep.

Okay, in the dream an angel says, "if you keep going, you can't go back."
Then I feel something pull me.

I've never told anybody. You think I'm nuts.
—Please don't get up. I'm afraid if you stand

it will end. Previously cached copy. No,
she doesn't think of him every day.
Some mornings she privileges freight trains and lilacs,
and thinks of a friend who said *lilac, lilac, lilac* is a train. Spring that's jewel-colored,

breakable. Yisborach v'yishtabach v'yispoar v'yisromam v'yismasay,
    v'yishador v'yis'aleh v'yisalal.
Morse code for end of contact. Stained glass in the chapel. Kadosh, kadosh,
    kadosh,

he hasn't pulled the trigger. We're on a safe tier—some delicate, spiny grillwork
in a closed system. Waiting for a Marconi communiqué, antennae strapped to
    kites. The star

envisions his children squirming around a funeral home,
which damn well should make him pause. A seeping of tone,
unrelated to the programmer's intent. Now what. Are we functional,

what could we do with the saved, and the unpulled trigger. With a preemptive
    configuration
and a new frame story, would he think of his ex-, or his new lover.
In Darwinian logic, changes come little by little
over vast intervals of time. To do this right

we should visualize a trigger. The general shape of a hook comes to mind,
but I can't help the image along. Although [delete if his mother is reading]

trigger finger inside me, and his tongue lolls me. Dangling off the bed, he looks
    up, smiles.
Insert paths here. The moment he paints compass points on his porch

so his kids can chose a hike whimsically. After a radio's unsnagged from an
    outlet
there's electric in the cord for one further sound. One more, and a seven
    second broadcast delay,
and he doesn't pull the trigger. Wireless blues played backwards, bedside candle
burning at sunup. A eulogy: words of praise, not necessarily for someone dead.
    Fell

holding hands. Because the time I knew him is short, spiral is troubled.
Ahead is a rotary of spinouts.

Resuming: it's hard to visualize the trigger finger.
    Around the stem of a paintbrush,
    rendering quasi-Audubon paintings of tigers and owls;
    encircling the focusing element of a microscope
    nearly daily in the most or less recent past.
    In a knot about to be pulled tight,
    holding ribbon's tension on giftwrap.
    Can't say for sure. Against rocks, a gull dashed him.

The image of the finger isn't going as planned. Do revamp the actuality, do,
of trigger pulled over heart, for this is where a writer or reader, outrageously self-absorbed,
is permitted to indulge. If that bitch hadn't lied to him. Do it now, back, and click.
Back, back, back,

a form of incantation. The precipices of a diagrammed sentence could put his verbs
on the Greenwich line. If I fly there. Get there. Stop loading. How does a fully blown heart look.

TIDING

Payphone mouthpiece speckles.   Called the alive boy.   I stand pixilated.
    One-hour processing,   three months dead. Over   and over
the sound gap   and failure.   Easy to see lapses   onshore,
    looking at drifting constructs.   All of us   little cases
    scampering after false constructs.   My latest emergency
has no valor.   My personal whatever   is not social witness, not political,
    could stay undeveloped   in a partytime throwaway camera.
Pointed, shot himself.   Whoops.   My late comfort smiling exactly to me,
his paparazzi.   His smile   I induced.   Who ever did care
    about the speaker?   Secretly, the avant-garde did.   Other photos
are in the vocative; all others are locators.   The personal epiphany,
    a petit mort.   I read Christine's poem of echolocation: *face is a*
    face...face...faces.   If I tell the alive boy   how the dead boy
gripped my shoulder,   looking to my dim eyes   rather than the meteor,
might feel unlost.   Live wire's voice wants to know   why I do this.
I am talking as a bat navigates.   Not to hear myself, but to know
    where I am.   Energy is usually flung   with selfish boomerang:
we want it returned.   Please be kinder.   Narrative or Language,
all bats,   longing for backlash.   As to know   the direction
of our faces.   If the dead   are soundwaves   something fronts us.

HER LOST DRAFT

The isn't of art.
Lose something every.
Lost door, hour badly spent.

Practice losing, losing.
You
travel. None will bring.

Watch. And look! my last, or
next-to-last, of three loved
went.

I lost
some realms I owned.
But it wasn't an Elizabeth.

(The joking voice.) Too hard
may look like (*Write it!*) like
One Art.

Hard to master, though it disaster,
the intent. Their loss. Accept
keys. Accept

the intent where it was meant.
Lost I: my mother's.
A disaster.

—Even losing You, I love.
I shan't.
Of losing:—the fluster.

LANDSCAPING

Where thought is a garden,
[ ]

[ ]
—Benjamin Friedlander, "Elegant Goo," *Partial Objects (series one)*

It is cacti lined up closely in a greenery like a tiny city.
It is sunset bouncing narrow avenues and coppery buildings. It's

Our Lady of the Tremendous Flower, painting *The Shelton with Sunspots,*
or she's shadebathing in the desert
by lying with her canvas
under the belly of her rust-free Ford.

It's Jenny Holzer. Or it's the Early Neon of Times Square trumped up,
superbulbed into a Singapore bright vista
with billboards that follow you—
a trait created by mating the Mona Lisa with the moon.

We, pedestrians, click click our feet;
image and text

change. Please watch me.
    And a one, two, three,
    two, two, three,
    this gesture

is the corps de ballet's Swan #24 B, or a city block at a regular interval.
This gesture is Baryshnikov hamming it up, or a fragment of Labanotation.
Gesture is a tilde, is airholes in a cello.
The cello is Man Ray's woman.
This gesture

is the swing of skyline as the N train nears Queens,
or the space between cacti.

[ ] is the gesture of Noguchi traveling
between Shikoku quarry and Astoria studio. Or the top of the head, flung.
Or the galore of maple leaves.

[ ] is the sexuality of stacked chairs, or trying on a stranger's hand-tailored
suit, or intimacy with New York City proper—
[Plant yourself on Union Square's lawn.
Subway vibrato will tunnel up through your sit bones.]

[ ] is love, or a gray ribbon, or a thin drama of shade thrown by a
saguaro—
[Fit your body
there.]

Please watch me.
[ ] is me at age three,

chalking an alley, bored on Long Island,
tucking my head as the neighbor's station wagon pulls over me—
I'm run over precisely between the wheels, so I won't be
rolled out, ribbed by tire treads like a saguaro. As inessential as the fruitless
peeing of lawn sprinklers.

[   ] is a thigh, or Fifth Avenue and Broadway vee'd by Steiglitz's Flatiron.
Straighten to the tallness of his photo, or to the port de bras of Arthur
    Mitchell, or basalt columns solid and hollowed, or the headline *NO*
    MORE SEPARATE SPHERES!
[   ] is Brecht

conveying sentences in stances, or the difference between American and Irish
    Sign Language.
    Shhh. Shhh. This gesture is shhh. This gesture is the pattern of the tile.
This gesture is
    you're in front of me. This gesture is
get out of town.
                [   ] is me

hiding in my twodoor in a state I can't explain, dislocation held by a vise.
Does a vise hold dislocation,

[   ] is a final couplet, or the arms of Venus di Milo,

or the empty set, or a birthdate, or plié,

or the guidelines in a viewfinder.

[   ] [   ] is a honeycomb.

[   ] is Noguchi's lyre for Graham's stage, is a flowering.

[ ] is wideness. Wideness is the span of skirt rippling
in Graham's arabesque *to the World.*

[ ] is Dickinson's dash, is jeté,
is a singing shape.

Three, two, three,
four, two, three; and a one.

HAPPY LIVING! A GUIDEBOOK FOR BRIDES

Cut-Outs For Creating
Your Own Furniture Arrangements
On Graph Paper:

(|)
48" extension table, [ ] [ ] {} {}
straight chairs, armchairs, | | |
a folding pictorial screen—,

dividing the room's global and lovely boys
from the dead one I still have a crush on.

All brackish winter, a widow tiara,
and rhinestones out there

in winded sandpockets.
One of the zesty girls photographs that

beach-nestled snow—cooing,
because there's offset stones, gray,

and she's a turpentine case.
Inside the next painter's studio I'm afraid

of blood from vials on canvases
though it's so remixable and replenishable,

beauty as it bricks turquoise.
A weapon to render living ovals.

Because I think the mortician put something flat
under my lover's sweater,

a new thorax. Blood as paint might replicate
flecked flesh, sudden suicide, sparse chest hair,

sudden sea spray—Motherwell
arcing and slamming brushes

on fiveply rag paper in Provincetown,
a series of oceansplashes the shape of Cape Cod

or the shape of asking something back.
Little progress to it, jogging on the beach.

Can't get warm or past the usual driftwood
on the curl that fists the Atlantic Ocean,

waves to Britain,
or to several docking pilgrims,

or to Motherwell's |‘(‘(|
—his thrusts of clumpy elegies, boyish inkblots.

Butterfly sticker
I stuck in the sweater cuff, lover

in coffin, wings larger than
the boxed body. An inability to fly

despite that good proportionality
of guts to wingspan.

LATIN ROOTS SUI AND CIDIUM

Under oneself. Tending, and does. Thinking only of one's hand.
Sui as in suitor—suing and pursuing.
To cede, which is withdraw. Sidelong. A glancing under decide.
Words get tired of melodrama and off themselves. Lying there, suitable.
An overuse of is, is, is. Sous as in under. Can you spare one under.
I haven't got a side. What it is: preventable. Ensuite. Or isn't—it's predisposed of.
Ici dieu. Where. Sous. You see. Non. Underneath veined cities.
Sweet seed, don't grow, don't, my sour sigh.

THE HEREAFTER HAS BEEN MODIFIED AS FOLLOWS

from the original version:
it has been formatted to fit your screen
and edited for content.

http://www. Myhereafter.org/god_hypertext
(a panorama of colorized wires, pretty fistful)

---------- Forwarded message ----------
>You are a landmass seen
>from an airplane. Your limpid bare ass is by the stream of your torso;
>on the stream there are moles,
>and those
>and those
>and those
>blooming moles are whole people. And the view
>from F 23 (window) is not a twinkling city; it is the inside
>of a calculator, opened watchback, dissection of a TV's bounceback.

The Gates of Prayer (Text Only)
this link is under construction

FAILURES OF LOVE.

For confusing love with lust
and [knock fist on chest] *pursuing fleeting pleasure at the cost of lasting hurt.*

For hiding from others behind an armor of mistrust
and [knock fist on chest] *the cynicism which leads us to mistrust the reality of unselfish love.*

We know You are somewhere off line, yet cannot name you. With our halting
human speech we say

G-d.

[Say Extra Things If the Holiday Falls on the Sabbath.]
[Double Click on the Icon
for Sabbath Link]

YOU MAY BE SEATED.

Act now—the gates are closing. Check out our special offer:
Two Names in the Book of Life for the Price of One

Press ENTER to process your contrition or CANCEL and your contrition will be erased.
Are you sure you want to cancel your act of contrition?
Yes, please cancel. No, please process.
Now processing....

Please enter the last four digits of your social security number.
Please enter your mother's maiden name.
Sorry, we cannot process your application at this time. Goodbye.

EMILY DICKINSON'S HOME PAGE—

In The Corner Of My Eye
A Safety Gate The World—

Note: This is an array formula and must be entered by pressing
CTRL+SHIFT+ENTER
+word +word +word.

THE KISS

Over ninety percent of all creatures kiss. Kissing is a landmark. Are we all programmed to put a kiss before a fondle? Glancing from eyes to lips: a Jungian kind of thing? Kiss-etiquette? The famous Klimt clasp-bodies are spun in gold paint euphoria. Doisneau's clinch is silver emulsion. Rodin's version, Francesca and Paolo, is a first kiss. Nude. Didn't know where to look at him—eyes, lips, eyes? He did not kiss although his hands had flown down my sides like the seams of a long dress, already grazed the length of me—crescents of my body—as I lay on carpet, and I'd already slept in the answering of his neck's nape. Did not.

FRACTAL

> *.... in search of the one word, often not even a rhyme, a word in the middle of a line; why—I don't know, but a word that absolutely ought to sound like ---, and mean ---! You know that. That's why I am driven toward you like a board against the shore.*
> —Marina Tsvetayeva in a letter to Boris Pasternak, mid-July, 1927

Sometimes one or more of us dreams the same thing.
A woman wearing asterisks on her earlobes

told me all dogs are commas.
Feline paws are therefores,

therefores are pyramids,
a cat sleeps like an @. And sits like an &.

Using an alt. key,
I'm setting my watch back a year.

That's as long as I'll consider you an option.
"Can't" "stand" "this." Bodies can lose the way

to tolerate annoyance:
grape weighing line, anything

without easy tear notches. Downwind of penciling
with loud graphite (only existentialists, at ponds,

have the right to print audibly)
my paraphrased smile only mimics

a distance. Such a warp. Truth:
I will wait for a word, tilting with long breaths

next to italics. We are myopic
but still magnetic, a qwerty of letters to each other.

Worse, better, or the same says the eye doctor. *When I take this away,*
worse, better, or the same? The flip-flip of lenses

blinks me. Quick:
let's look at the same brightness,

then close our eyes and watch again.
I've wanted to see what is on your screen. Buying into

the control/option/shift world
where computers give a person

what a person wants:
two dots over a you,

easy to install brackets, sic-sic,
and hyphens connected—

if I am reading aloud
you maybe don't get the full effect.
Is this line break or

this stanza break equivalent, lengthwise, to two periods?
A caret allows us to add, above a line,

the forgotten. Example:
sporadic days in love
^. In the epoch

between slippery and sketchy
we make a third thing.

LOOKING FOR DELIGHTS

It's hard to remember why

he wrote a poem
for Robert Bly—

Bly, who thinks
nothing is more boring than language poetry.

Poetry spits
at B.F. Skinner.

If some create categorgalia
then I'll never see Pavarotti sing with the Spice Girls

which Pavarotti did (shaking those vibratos out of his big head
while the Spices shook the plunges of their pantsuits).

Upon a time Art lost Author, The Viewer took over
and you're on our list.

Still, still, the world of narrative and small gestures.
Too many abst-

Too many abst-, abst-,
(we're on planet mars) (hi)—because: heard an interviewer say

fragmentations are the only way some women can find their voices.
        Look, lost my that.   My female drop-stitching.

Some frou-frou. As if
rejection of free white verse is women's work.

I had a teacher, when he liked to write some poems,
he just liked to write some goddamn poems—

THERE IS NO TOWARDS

No *S.*

Dear Molecule:

My character, inside this screen, I might scream, we all might, I might, inside
out, swapping with you—to-live-ward,

no, stct, no,

verge, musty darling, come away, to-dead-wards, der Tod, out of your wake,
untoward,
away from this page. Verge well toward, /baby,
turn around, /and let me see that sexy body go /*bump bump bump.*
J-Boog, Raz-B,

Lil' Fizz, Omeran and OED: The suffix
-wards includes the notion of the manner
as well as the direction of the movement,

&-*wards* expresses a definite direction and it is in contrast
with all other directions,

like forwards. Like fromwards. *Bump bump bump.*
Sending this out to all the sexy daddies. Wanna
get with you. Baby show me, baby turn around,

and let me see that sexy body go
bump bump bump. Casper, cross over, atoms star-distance-apart.
Be a big vulnerable star, so hot-to-death, da bomb. Puff up, like a sudden owl.
Yeah,

when the body goes
I'll spin the decompose diffuse tight energy
MC squared, P. Diddy, oh croup croup,

the Molecule's young 'un   at age two. Does he have the croup?
The Molecule sits with the child, they breathe   in the steam,   in the shower,
check it out, is it the croup?   Croup, croup?   Baby, croup, croup?

Molecule Martian, word, plural toward,   to-outerspace-colonies-wards.
M. believed in such. The choice

between toward and towards is determined by euphony, so
thou be conscience-calmed—see here it is—I hold it towards—turn around,

toward me, grapheme willin' and the creek don't rise. Shake it,
shake it, all crust and incarnations, no living hand. Oh /He

died on the road /Oh, he
died on the road /Never had no money
to pay for sufficient clothes /

Hello, in the window! Are we so apart, ghost?
        You know I like it when your body goes—
/it's a question of time. /But
        Depeche Mode isn't growing on me, dear. Abc-ya, my sunshine, disperse
the sunshine, your leather jacket lurks on my in-bed-breasts. What was with
        leaving your jacket on the bed? Remember? No, I miss, no, you

goose, give up the ghost, don't hang with other ghosts   at the vectors
        of change.
Lose that body, shake it, let me see that sexy body go   *bump bump bump.*
        Toward space. Oh you   were a friend of mine.   Oh he
never done no wrong /I stole (I stole)

I stole away and cried /
        /And every time   I hear his name /

                /He   was a friend of mine.

Dear Search Committee:

Since the death of a beloved
my aesthetic has changed. My new work
is perhaps traditional or epiphanic
in its use of a consistent narrative
(the thread of my loved one's death).

Dear *S*:

Do your own narration.

Dear Page:

I hate you. The intentionality of this container
can be moved to strike. The artificiality too.

Wooshik says *a rat-tat-tat-tat is an echo in your voice.*
A ding-a-ling-a-ling is a song for your house. This house

is a continuous present—hello there, Molecule,
leaning out the window. In the context of

context this page is loud hooey. I would like to
meet some sentences more honest than these,

someone to fray silence with gentle fray. I met
someone, Molecule, but the creek rose. My shining thwart, brimming

and slaying—jealous? But I see right through
to you. Baby turn around

and let me see that sexy body go/*bump bump bump./*
C'mon /Let's go /

C'mon /Let's go /
It's pandemonium, baby.

WHAT LISA THINKS

no wings no harp   *especially when I'm walking*

&

DEATH AND SAUCEPAN

I step outside

to access haunting, who might be
a number of simmering molecules.
Should I see you
in the sand dunes? My darling? The sky and ocean have been appointed
enough, even in the Ashbery scapes—

but a man who is living
asks tenderly as an unforgotten pelvis
why I agree the shore scruff before sundown

is magic-magic blue. Why
call anything anything; ditch
tenderly and unforgotten
into dusky brush at Junction 6

to Cape Cod, a scorpion tail—its tip
far shot into Eastern Standard Time. Thus sundown
is early and arachnid, but the just-before blue,

guttering blue, nearly makes me unashamed
to say (up and around other lines)
hell, bloody hell, look over there.
Atop gruesome faith in imagery
a bay that's not silk, not chiffon,
just liquidy enough to arouse, a stretch,
a lycra of blue, *merille*, metallic as a body gasping
below mentionable clouds. Sliver. Vibrant

papercut, close to silver, opens little
but brings me closer to you—whose blood
was correction fluid flooded over.

I yanked my one shock-white hair, scalp to split end.
It looked like floss—
luster white as a lit bulb bared in a mirror.

Hopkins wrote *shining from shook foil.* I am dead too, so that last bit was extra.

SLEEP PATTERNS

(She doesn't appear to be moving. But she's got this tremor. It's just a very slow tremor. You could see it if you used time-lapse

photography.)

Enter Hamlet.
Dive Ophelia.

Stoke her pillows. She'll synchronize, set the alarm as you wish, remove one arm from her body to get her chest closer to you. She's allowing for things, but she's not sure she'll stay. With you, or in general—in world. Surrounded by Dolby (last credit, this movie). Someone ought

to convulse around you
five minutes more.

She needs
procrastinating time. A nap's a border

a couch is closer to
a country undiscovered (that we wait up for);

you can sleep lightly
through the crochet of a throw.

Hey, would you like a lovescone?
May I tuck you in with a perchance?

Boom. The girl will get up. She will. To look at the weather, right away. She's a sprint sleeper—with all lights on and door unlocked. Because: she's sleeping faster than anyone. Because: she's rising at rooster hours. Even her resting pulse is cocked. Some hearts zzzzz

"uh oh"
are unable

to unstutter from bird thirty-six
to bird five hundred beats per minute—

unrousable, you see. Just in there, a little
nest made of computer paper perforations.

Fact: lots of hummingbirds
die in their sleep. If one

pierced a vein on my arm,
(now it's me talking) sweetly....

HeartInfo Question and Answer Line (partial text)

A: Vasovagal [pronounce like Bagel] Syncope.
The heart's controlled by two types of nervous systems.
[Doesn't it seem like more?]

Overactivity in one
slows the heart.

Less blood to veins.
You'll faint.

Oph. Blown youth.
Sing a-down a-down.

Ham. I loved you not;
a thousand natural shocks.

Venipuncture is a trigger stimulus to avoid.
Also, syncope may occur in crowded situations. Spells are brief. Retinas—

I'm not afraid of needles.
I didn't say it was a phobia. It's a biological response.

Protects the body?
There isn't any research about that.

I always mix up melanin with melatonin.

Something about a fever—

What does it mean: Mercury in retrograde? Sun sleeps. Venus waits fervently; that arrow in her left ventricle makes her dizzy. There's a loop de loop every sixty-nine days around the sun, or something. I'm not sure how it might affect us. If something weird happens, remember
—well.

There are backup disks.

(Her tremor's so slow, it appears she is reaching,

hello?)

REPLACING A THRESHOLD

....They can come from anything and anywhere....The plane is not on a surface, but on a plane which is imagined. It moves in a mind. It is not there physically at all.
—Philip Guston

At a scuba-dive wedding,
the underwater bride holds up an "I Do" sign
to the underwater groom.
She's concerned, because in order to show
the "I Do" side
she must flip the dorsal "I Do Not"
toward herself.
These sound-images are various, are
divers. Erstwhile,

signifiers shift their inclines, buzzing like Cessnas,
lifted by sundry helium balloons into the eaves of doorways.
Home Depot says *If the threshold is too tight, you can plane down the door*
or lower your threshold. A door that's not used as a door

is a tabletop resting on file cabinets. In my home, anyways.
We are anywhere: in between a *Rio Rose* color chip
and Guston's *Table Top,* 1979. Nabokov is sure, so sure

a lower case "m" is pink, a fold of pink flannel.
But *slight differences may occur* between color remembered
and actual paint when applied to a surface. In *Table Top*
the sound-image of a chair floats
through a color called *French Lavender* by Ace Hardware,
Pink Inkling by Glidden Interior.
The chair is an ideal chair and simultaneously
an imitation that won't hold your sit.
Where there could be vinyl or plush, instead
there's a plunge, another plane, a pink swivel,

the tundra of my mouth breaching pasteboard skies,
but not drinking any,
my lips *Ragged Chiffon* over stucco instead of *Rose Kiss*
in a high gloss for walls and trim. After reciprocating saws,
and too little back and forth,
what are people doing with their salvage? We are anything, ocean hobos
piecing together paint-swatches: *Raspberry Touch. Azure Afternoon.*
The plane we're on is a seesaw,
so how shall we walk one toward another? Is that
half a shoe on Guston's table? The arbitrary relationship

between the signified and the sign
eschews closed systems and Gulf Streams
so hair that isn't brick or firetruck or cherry
can still be called red,

as in abandon, as in a declension:
the barrio, the baha, the bahamas.
There are skyphones all around us

during the revolutions and rotisseries of partnered sleep.
This lamp's bead-chain
descended from anywhere. Pull it.

END OF SPELL

I'm in the zone of: Who Are You? And in this Twilight
it's hard to remember there were birdies, flowers in a hand basket,
eyes made, a breeze touching my left cheek and your right ear
in one swoop. So trippingly.
                                        My good judgment.   Where?

A hell in the basket. I want to sweep you
for my fingerprints. Give them back.

And before we make ritualistic exchanges—
your boxers for my umbrella—
I want to tape wires to you
and ask you things.
I believed

I'd been reading your forehead—
neon letters running across, announcements
plain and big: *I'm falling*   *in*   *with you.*
Anticipating strokes you desired,

and applying them,
thought I knew something.
Maybe all we had in common
was the way we conduct.

North is not even North.
No one will give you equal shivers, honey.

THE URGE TO SAY

any odd sound. Any odd name.
Doctor Carl Bennett has Tourette's Syndrome.
He says some names are candy for the mind.
He hoots *Babaloo Mandel, Floyd Flake.*

Doctor Carl Bennett has Tourette's,
phonic tics: echolalia and palilalia.
He hoots *Babaloo Mandel, Floyd Flake.*
All these railings.

Phonic tics—echolalia and palilalia:
the repeating of single words, ends of sentences (yours, someone else's).
All these railings
along the staircase of disorder.

The repeating of single words, ends of sentences
is something to hold on to.
Along the staircase of disorder
synapses of logic firefly.

Something to hold on to:
associations lapping over memory.
Synapses of logic firefly.
I try to control my breathing.

Associations overlap memory.
Which aspects of metabolism are controllable?
I try to control my breathing,
then forget how to breathe entirely.

Which aspects of metabolism are controllable?
Nothing's as easy as pasta.
I forget how to breathe. Entirely.
Sometimes a door calls out, says

nothing's as easy as pasta.
Lately words stop sounding like words.
Sometimes a door calls out, says:
Turn back, I may not be locked.

Lately words stop sounding like words.
Words words words words words. Allure.
Turn back. I may not be locked.
As if I were chattering Echo: you say it first.

Words words words words words. Allure—
jump off an overpass? Roll in the leaf pile?
As if I were chattering Echo: you say it first.
How can I control the tumbling urges to

jump off the overpass, roll in the leaf pile,
say I love you when I don't love you.
How can I control the tumbling urges to
shout involuntary phonations into heat ducts,

say I love you when I don't love you
yet. I'll scratch the ache in my throat,
speak involuntary phonations into heat ducts,
blurt out vocal tics. Just

scratch the ache in my throat.
Some names are candy for the mind.
Blurt out vocal tics, just
any odd sound, any odd name.

THE ONLY UNIVERSAL TONGUE

Who gets to be the man? grew increasingly irrelevant,
replaced by *who am I really, now that I'm with you?*
—from the "Brown Boys" chapter of *Taboo* by Boyer Rickel

1. *LOCAL OVERTURE*

Music is an intimate at first brush. Music is,
when you want it, graspable as your own chest. On
the soundbar of your sternum—feel the slipped bass.
Where is your surge protector? Double, double, tinfoil treble.
Spacey antenna. Gracenote bubble. Warmups like mei me my mo moo.
May I have this dance?— a doffing of waltz, among the brazen decibels,
with a borrowed libretto. I've heard you somewhere before.

2. *INCANTATA STOLEN FROM GEORGE OPPEN'S* "OF BEING NUMEROUS"

"Chorus (androgynous): 'Find me
So that I will exist, find my navel
So that it will exist, find my nipples
So that they will exist, find every hair
Of my belly, I am good (or I am bad),
Find me.'"

3. *BALLAD in honor of BRANDON of San Francisco*

Amy's day-old wedding ring
diamond glows in the black light

Amy's blissful upon her husband
dropping us off at "Stud"

she doesn't feel the ridiculous dynamic
between us versus

the only other woman here
that woman wearing less

that woman dancing all wavy, like an infinity sign
that woman surrounded by bodies

oh, but my savior,
my pixie, elfin fairy

Pan in Hawaiian shirt
spikey hair boytop

let's drink to him, put him in a snifter
imagine the poking of his boxers

look at the evolving
space between dancers

praise underage Brandon,
who took me

as his song after song dance partner

4. *ARIA DA CAPO in the KEYSTONE STATE*

At autumn's end, in a tiny valley,
the tweed grays of naked trees blur toward a blue
stained and bleached like a collar. Uppity chicks are whistling while they work.

New York City? says a voluptuous transsexual in a very red dress.
I could never live in a place like that. As if a man, I look her up and down—
that pleases her. She gestures, saying *these*
grew and grew on my hormone therapy; I can hardly jog.
We are two girly-girls on barstools.
We stand to hug goodbye. She looks me up and down. I don't know if I'm pleased.

She tells me *oh, you're just a tiny thing* with a musky remorse for her immutable build.

I want to be a man. Not a tiny thing. In the straight bar
one guy repeats and repeats *Hey, I'm talking to you*. Tiny thing. He says
Think you're high class or something? Tiny thing. I say *Fuck off.*
A hero type says *leave the girl alone*, and even the famous
You wanna take this outside? Tiny thing. Hero
buys me a beer. But I fantasize about a punch thrown
by the gay bar's contralto in the very red dress.

Oh, that great big beautiful doll, could I count on her allegiance?

5. CREDO for the DRAG QUEEN named OHSOFONDA BOYZ

Freedom is a breakfast tour

that meets in front of the Queen Anne Hotel
a Victorian Painted Lady

Freedom is the Blue Line to Alcatraz
the ferry's wake is a vine of thick shaving cream

Have you ever been to a drag show? asks Ohsofonda. *What are you doing here?*
Ohsofonda points out *That's Chablis in the white and she's okay*

Ohsofonda vanishes momentarily
to perfect her bosom's duct tape

her song blares—
Vogue, vogue, vogue

what are she and I
when she is light and alluring in my lap

and then, the moment she's been waiting for
the brother she hasn't seen in three years walks in

he growls *this is my "real" woman*
referencing his wife on his arm

then he soaks up Budweisers at the bar
I hate him with every bone

but Ohsofonda, impeccable queen,
as a woman, she forgives, she dances

SOMETIMES A SEPTUM ALMOST DEVIATES

and a nose becomes a bird. It doesn't seem to mind. This isn't real. There's no flying.
There's a kind of hush all over the world. The whoosh of a sneeze is a cluster of feathers.

Lipstick on polyester is yuck. I saw it, but gave you my true blood today.
We're plush nothing, there's a lawn mooning for us,

it's mowed low. In restaurants, the grass is always greener on the other plate,
has hash browns for example. The plate says:
You can have it all when she's done. Do I represent your desire?
Look at how you're a hawk.

This is part of a loved poem: *i like my body when it is with your body.*
She to he: *only when I'm with you.* Oh, you can sometimes see part of a bird's reflection
on pupils or on patent leather or on a black car.

Why are you wearing swimming trunks in bed? Later, arms are dreaming.
Can they dream if they're not pinned? Hush now, wait now, we're completely *unfinished.*

LETHAL

Mistletoe is a parasite. Subsists in lust. On palo verdes—desert trees. Tiny *on the wall, who's the fairest* berries full of poison stud the riot of stems. *Loves me, loves me not.* Like daisy petals, the lure's in the luck lurking quiet. Fatal fruits. Should I stop, count each berry so I'll know if any fall? Cat mustn't eat. Pinned above my bedroom's entry a fresh, looped french twist looms: covenant of bewitch. Mistletoe's no hedge—cover me, pagan. Permission's running rampant in our veins. Allow lips a full-on plea. Botanists won't know hot growth from host tree.

TEMPLE GRANDIN'S SQUEEZE MACHINE

Temple cares for cattle, holds a PhD in Animal Science, is autistic. Her jeans practically rip with empathy as she visits sites, bends to stroke before the slaughter. Agricultural Physics and Engineering are her life's work. She creates blueprints in her mind, easily, seeing every detail of structures shaped like linked seahorses. The curved ramps and opaque fences she designs for abattoirs let cows retain their innocence. Each cow, unaware of human intention, approaches the unseen captive bolt stunner, approaches calmly.

Temple tells chute operators the cows should be held—not tentatively, but firmly—as a final quiet gesture. But Temple herself barely tolerates the embrace of a human. Savant, she cannot stand the swirl of emotions a person emanates: they are overwhelming, as she computes them. Temple analyzes such feelings. Surveyed, it's all gibberish. The embrace is a noose—she's cattle, roped. A hug traps her in terror, skittish senses ravaged by stimuli, autism rendering her nearly incapable of bearing touch.

Wanting a hold she could endure—something like a cattle chute—Temple designed herself a Squeeze Machine: her vice without the human. Upholstered, V-shaped, it's hooked to an industrial compressor. She controls the pressure, the time involved. Oliver Sacks visited Temple and tried the machine. It reminded him of deep sea diving: *The pressure of water on my diving suit as whole body embrace.*

Temple doesn't squirm in her Squeeze Machine. Nor is she left undone. Inside the squeeze she thinks of love. The device itself helps her to conceptualize this emotion. She calls herself an anthropologist on Mars.

How long is the perfect embrace? Perhaps when neither lets go first. Or when the climax of being held is felt by both at the same time. There are T-shirts that list reasons why a beer is better than a woman, a cucumber better than a man—embraces replaced, simplified. I heard a dancer named Erica Blue say: *If I had three arms I'd hug you two and a half times.*

There are strange magnets on the tips of hipbones and centers of clavicles. *You* becomes *sweet embraceable you.* Against the instinct to shy away.

CANCER HAS NOT SEEDED–

the cells are localized. Tiny talons fastened to my mother's uterine lining. So tiny that she bans me from flying home surgery day, but slides a *Last Will and Testament* and *Do Not Resuscitate Instructions* into a manila envelope. Propped, for me to find, in her refrigerator next to perishables. To her, that's the way you do things, you do things "in case." Who am I to let my thoughts get scary because she's also bought a cemetery plot and says *I love you.*

She calls from Long Island Jewish, jaunty as John Glenn going up a second time, says *I love you*—again. *Oh these people, I'm waiting, they're behind* she's telling me, as if waiting for nothing more than a haircut, which she never does, though, since she cuts her own.

If she could keep me, someday, from knowing she died, maybe waiting until she actually died, then sending messages from beyond like *I might die* or *I've begun to die* or *I'm a little bit dying now,* that's how she'd handle it. She's always been a handler, chopping vegetables before letting repairmen in our house—an excuse to open the door with a knife in hand to protect the small daughter I was, and herself.

Tradition of control thus instilled, I track my mother's anesthetized transit from hospital wing to hospital wing as if she has a homing device on her ankle. The surgeon recognizes my voice (it is my mother's) on the phone. So demanding questions don't surprise him. He offers *She has her own way of doing things.* Her voice is completely colorless, twenty-four hours later, when she calls me collect and says *I think I need help.*

Your ragdoll heart, after twenty-eight years of never hearing that, would crash out of its cradle too. Yes, the cancer is localized and has already been thrown in the river, and nobody thinks it likely to swim back, but yes, you'd lean forward in an attempt to be aerodynamic and you'd visualize a gas pedal on the airplane floor and slam it.

I string overnight flight to subway to taxicab. *Oh*, she says as I hurry into her room. She moves her sewn body on the bed, making room for me. And she says *Are you all right? I love you. Don't I sound better now? Lie down. You should take a nap. I really love you. Have this juice.*

DIARY

The opposite of striking him.
It is gawky to say.
Speech, a loose tooth.

That I'm in love I can't.
Wasps and wisps of words. My minutiae sentiments
could make your mind pruney. What if I fixate

on a M.O.M.A. Pollock, *Echo,* till drip lines
are dozens of shoelaces, tipped with lacquer and raging.
Daily strands: *Me, too, I...* or *That reminds me of...*

Angling. Gawky, really gawky with *this is where I went* and *what I did.*
When I am the conversationalist
the less patient fixate on a point

by my voile head. Mental pushpins scrape me:
the bored post notes.
Wholly detached listeners cast documents

right over my face, cutting and pasting text.
I myself concentrate on a speaker's lock of hair
just so I'm not waiting to chime.

As I was saying. When he held me, I was not a boring person.

Embarrassing, the need to peep, this saturation.
Forgive me. One I adore absorbs
my excess speech (her eyeglasses solar panels).

Another I adore fields my prattle
despite her burning focaccia. All my talking
and I forget to charge the cordless. One who is

my poet-cousin—whom I also adore, and
shortly I would like to say more about her—
finds humor in that juiceless telephone.

Through my answering machine, gleeful-sweet:
I feel helpless because I can't hear you! Now I add
there is a gallantry to her poems.

I can't not say: the particulars of his handholding.

MADE OUT OF SIXES

Crisscrossing can be messy: tangled puppet strings. But this eclipse
is tidy—a moment of alignment in the do-si-do planets weave.
Tonight, earth makes moon blush ruddy. They are eye to eye;

> an embarrassment of sunrays collects on lunar surface. Interlocking
> orbit points, a classic hook-up. Which planet initiates the echo,
> earth ringing before moon? Should we know the dancer from the dance?

Or is the moon's brightening glance, slowly unshadowed, a dance
of shape within shape, boundaries within and without? An eclipse
is round swallowing round, longing in unselfed language—like Echo's

> declarations. Twains finally meeting. Strange pearl in a weave
> knit by the ellipses planets slide on—a sexy, otherworldly interlocking,
> va va voom. Perhaps it's mere déjà vu (in the moon's eye)

when a spot, inky as the dilated center of an eye,
covers the moon, an iris. Eclipses are tropes; each dance
embodies the overlap of meanings. This interlocking,

> unlike synecdoche, is whole symbolizing whole. Eclipse,
> you're yin to yang as one, the Aristophanes Sandwich we've
> meant to recreate, (one slice of bread the echo

of another—sliced next to each other). Greco-
Asian philosophy aside... moon enters wholly into the umbra, foci
fuse in earth's conical shadow, and orbit nodes weave.

Slow crossing is sky T'ai-chi: palm passing palm. Sway, pendants—
you have world enough to admire each other. An eclipse
creates a hybrid planet, creates a malapropism. Interlocking

words obscurate each other, hybrid as eclipses in certain interlocking
poetic forms. Now, as shadow swaggers over moon, do you hear the echo
of discs changing, one riff untangling from another? Eclipse

comes from the Greek for *omit*. It's about stealing away from the eye,
then returning; the part of a starlit highwire dance
that makes us gasp although the spotlight is on us. Weave

a story, Eclipse, as you have done since dawn: Moon-god pulling the weave
of his cloak over his head, moon trying to sleep. Interlocking
myths—dragon clutching the moon, or other trickster—dance.

Awe approaches fear; our wide mouths echo
a history of reactions. Yet unlike solar eclipses (which the naked eye
cannot tolerate, and have signified the world's end) a lunar eclipse

is less rare, lulling. And in the lull an eclipse weaves
dilating eye receives moon fully, interlocking
with the penumbra. Pupil and iris echo the unled dance.

TO LISA: WE DESCEND FROM WORRIED MOTHERS

There's a story you tell. Each time it's told
cowboy boots are mentioned, and dancing,
dancing as a form of optimism.
Later I hear the boots were magenta.
The boots were oxblood.
Oxblood might be red with kick.
It's easy to convey a narrative,

or no, elaboration must carefully begin with a painting

underneath a painting. We are pale mortal bodies
tossing back Yuenglings and chicken wings,
foraging through an iceberg salad at a location called Tavern.
I can reject pathos.
You can reject the cold canvas that's stripped of the lyric.
Something has to burst, someone must be humane enough

to hold lines physically and recite them to me in my Buick.
Please trust, my friend, my pessimist, what you love,
so I can visit

and make bootleg copies.
I listen from afar
while you defend the possibility
of a theorem that reveals
the common properties of masterpieces.
I am afar as afar can be a lot of the time. I watch

as your sweetheart speaks to you
and a new shade of amber invents itself.

There are sudden solaces
that have no known place of manufacture,
that come to us at reasonable cost.
I want to see more

the way you do.

SONNETS AFTER JOEL MEYEROWITZ ASKS OUR QUESTION

Photographing the new beauty:
Statue of Parabola, metal piazza, metal fauna exposed,

metal acquiring a nudity. The rubble is bony is
limitless as the Vatican basement's silk thread collection—

index of color possible, shelves and shelves of spectrum
the sisters use in tapestry restoration. Forgive me,

I'm a sinner looking on and on. A photographer I know,
not Meyerowitz, careened to the site, alive, his gold cross skidding

clavicle and lightheaded arousal. Hid in an EMS truck
and rode into the stench library. But who can Trump

the blown aesthetic? Somewhere's a picture
of me on the glassy Winter Garden bridge,

taken in the Twentieth Century. Later do we slip home,
sleek, reaching down, on a romantic plane—

one hand drops.
Splay and blossom,

rosy, pocket full of ash. Grove of cranes.
Manual raking in lieu of machines

whenever a body part is found. I will be
utilitarian and barbaric.

I decided while listening to Meyerowitz's interview.
Forthright, sublime 8x10 negatives:

grainless and disinterested enough
for hellish pink haze. Or I decided

while talking to the sun. Out of the
lyric's debris. In the lower deck lanes, GW Bridge,

my car's bike rack a furtive skyline:
bicycle handlebars jutting—

out of the eruv

of wires and sea walls.

This is a switchyard

for aesthetic railcars

unhooking.

Out of radiance

that eats your eyes.

Red radiating.

Don't say Pompeii.

If I remove content

what will I put in?

A corroded, universal line.

In such dust you can see the record of flight.

RECONSTRUCTION WITH ORIGINAL FRAGMENTS

Even after every dream he dies again. Hands streaming
back, without one more fondness for the road. The crux of streets
still crosses all wrong. In water and light

crossed waves are cancelers. Plunging water can be counteracted by a crest—
waves love other waves' hollows. Crossed light waves of the primary colors
is color goodbye, a suicidal shine, white.

A painting with one stroke missing can live. One stroke
stolen and isolated and made new
and shot from an airbrush. You press the color.
You switch parts from airgun to airgun,

rearticulate the brushstroke, you
(mirror mirror
who's the postmodernist)
manipulating a painting that already happened. You

press the color. We roam another museum. You point out
the small gape in the flesh, the heads in the Caravaggio
peering at Jesus' injury. Paling light
descending under Berlin's low clouds. Here we enter

the American sector. Here we go. Here we pick up
the small gape in the history.
Here, now, must we really keep mapping event over event,
a Checkpoint of events, a crux of streets, hands

streaming back? On the way
to museums with their original reliefs: music. In the streets we pass music.

It's too romantic to say *we*. It's too light to say *on the way*. In the midpoint of
    our walk
patches of music sweep into each other. The Dead Zone
between musics is a walkable mesh segue of accordion into flute—

a wack combination only perceptible in equidistance. It's hard
to find the frequency. You press the color. The color is thinking of

a bit of marble arm, or leg, or wing in the reconstructed Pergamon frieze.
O isolated wing, torn. O fragmentation and
packing tape. Strap impulses together. Steal, with an airgun,

glossy porcelain figurines. Looped and released
from their museum vitrines, they gather
beneath your extracted, crossbred, post-post brushstroke,
a paint streamer wide as the figurines, a brushstroke lifting from its sources

like a limb. You press the color. You switch parts. You reverse
death. Now there is a merry-go-round of figurines, round and round,
not in chronological order. It's reunification. You are gone

and here I am, speaking to you, not to my dead engraved love.
A diptych of hollows, one of us swept into the other of us. Fleshy light
in our most meager crevices. Light truing the fit.

APOLOGY IS RED UP LIKE THIS:

in shorthand, without accoutrements,
and the hull of
this word is
made in a shipyard.

During the final Ice Capades, known as the *Wisconsin Stage*, words grew
formations:
prefixes and connotations. John Robert Gregg,
1888, crafted a shorthand

essentializing curvatures
of commonly used sounds.
Diamond Jubilee's Gregg Shorthand Textbooks
helped thousands of married women
who left the job [the job] years ago
reenter the secretarial field.

Seventy-six tombolos led the slim parade.
Connecting islands—oh so fra-
gile—Fra Angelico annunciating,
fff space, tab tab tab, fff space
tab tab tab.

A secretary's speed is measured in syllables.
Sounds uttered by the dictator
are broken into syllables: *I'm the commander—*
see, I don't need to explain—
I do not need to explain why I say things.
That's the interesting thing about being the president.

Apology is red
up like this:
its inside (aside) becomes its out (beside)

and so apology's got
one of the freshest insides around.

It's OK that a word is a placeholder.
The place is on a conveyer belt,
a chorus-assembly line only for its one self.

> Words' spines tremble
> like earbones. There's just
> a spot of rubbing on the spine of apology,
> and even fainter sunning to the spine's cloth. Sweetie, there's foxing
> at the upper edge, apology's internally foxed,
> with surface dirt, and yet
> it is of value, rare and not usually found in valuable condition.
> The chipping across the top edge does not affect the text.
> Nor, of course, does the hint of lamination.

The Unnamable in near fine condition!
The Unnamable sunned but crisp!
Apology, you're a classic in your fine dust jacket.

Words don't like their pictures taken.

Peep at words. They will let you touch for three quarters.

Apology is red
            up like this:

scoured capillaries,
clean as new PVC,
flayed in layers.
Not Plath's lampshade—

you misunderstand.
Apologized for naught.
My face at apology's hull.

Struggled to remember the shape of apology. Used a counterfeit for so long.
Longhandedly sought a scalloped apology with a compression valve. Cut
        apology in half,
then died. Death says: apologize. No I won't. If you don't you are grounded.

Let apology be red
        objects like this:
plastic shells. Not dropped.

        Apologie we are so proud. The dead, lightbulbs, cracked.
        Crusade without Congressional offspring. In bumper sticker.

Ready? Here, apology based on the equation for a propeller.
Apology banks, changing the angle of its feathers. One mile past apogee
all apologies are unjustified, use extra curlicues and have no edge
to reach. Apology walks into a
can't see that line.

Gregg Shorthand represents vowels as hooks and circles on consonants.
Words have portals and each portal leads to hypertext
so you can see what might happen. Here is Beckett's apology:
I am sorry for our lack of comprehension.
Apology can break open to polo or log.

Words produce dunes; a dune's (inside (is (like (a (word's (((((
A word's inside is grainy & genderless (0 (0 (0(. Not vaselike.
Inside a word is *oar* and outside is *would.* ((((((((((w(OarOuld.))))))))))

So we paddle. Inside of inside is a puddle.
As more sides are added new meanings can slip.

Words are not boxed,
their insides don't fit inside—
mine neither.

Typewriting and shorthand are my keys to the work force today.
88gg--
The thickness, length and position of strokes are all significant.
Apology, after stroking, can become a tombolo. All I have

are the most peculiar letters,
the round and the dangly.
I offer them without suffix or pretense. Not idealized—don't you think it—
though:
it's tautless such and such
so underdone, what a production number,
sung out-out-out—
not rewarding as wish'd. If you would like a free upgrade—

Sunny, hunker, no beach umbrella, solemn love for the idyllic gulled scene,
solemn belief in the small crop circles surrounding the beach grass patches—

if beach grass, beach roses, beach la la la could hold the page together, no
trembling,
we couldn't get anywhere.
You just want something to think about, don't you?
Vacant. Only inside once.

Said he'd rather fff space tab tab tab than sit in that uncomfortable chair.
There's no way to repeat that. Your moraine moraines.
Paper flopping over the typewriter,
the breeze is sounder, sounding.

Apology's inside is protected by the overhang of its letters.
The vine around apology makes it diligently tentacled.
Apology, as the absence of what ought to be, lolls in place (can hardly keep its
place).
Nobody knows if apology is filled with silt.

Here is Eliot's apology: 'getical cats.

How a word is affected by its use:
in dormant states a word's inside gets more liquefied—
since a word's inside is
already liquid
its liquid state
is past liquid.

Words arrived in boxes.
We recycle the boxes.
Can't flip
over to the map
as if seeking the key to Whitman
or Godiva chocolates. Bonbons
and not so bons. Cracked.

I apologize for the fickle
and unlexical. Let apology be
for whim cycles. Synecdoche your umbrella.

FAX TO E.E. CUMMINGS

If god is just a few
semicolons, hinted at by Hebrew

shorthand, we're
dots on a die. We drag lips.

Why my lover's eyelashes:
a spirituality

meant to sting;
each I think
is a parenthesis

altogether
they batter.

Pine needles,
a throw of I-Ching lines

pricking the voodoo of me.
If consciousness is only electricity,

I quit. Fly.

Bees play the meander
route of sipping.

I want random;
i want i don't know

NOTES

The book's epigraph is from "Articulation of Sound Forms in Time" (*Singularities*) by Susan Howe.

"Landscaping" is indebted to Benjamin Friedlander's pronunciation of a bracket as "blank" and to Boyer Rickel.

"*Happy Living! A Guidebook for Brides*" references a book with the same title and paintings by Anthony Viti.

"Fractal" borrows from "Bright Show" by Eric Burger and Brenda Hillman's lecture "Alternative Punctuation in Contemporary Poetry" and her comment that an ampersand is "a pregnant woman doing yoga."

"Looking for Delights" is for Jon Anderson.

"Replacing a Threshold" was commissioned by the Scottsdale Museum of Art.

"The Urge to Say" and "Temple Grandin's Squeeze Machine" are indebted to Doctor Carl Bennett, Professor Temple Grandin, and Oliver Sacks (*An Anthropologist on Mars*).

"Sometimes a Septum Almost Deviates" is after poetry by Kate Rosenberg.

"Made Out of Sixes" is for Tenney Nathanson and is a response to his class "Close Reading Poetry."

"Diary" is for Barbara Cully, Jennifer Rosen Heinz, and Jane Miller.

"Reconstruction with Original Fragments" is after the painting "Porcelain Stroke" by Eckhard Etzold.

"Apology Is Red up Like This" reflects *Apology Brooch* from *The Shorthand Series* by Rebecca Strzelec and Kat McLellan's wish for a word with an inside.

Deborah Bernhardt received a BA in English/Art History/Photography from Sarah Lawrence College and an MFA in Creative Writing from the University of Arizona. She has been a fellow at the Fine Arts Work Center, Provincetown, a Jay C. and Ruth Halls Fellow at the Wisconsin Institute for Creative Writing, a Writer-in-Residence at Penn State Altoona, and a recipient of a Literary Arts Grant from the Wisconsin Arts Board. She lives in Baraboo.